HOW TO FIND
& CALL A NEW
PASTOR

Robert J. Strand

Another in the series...

PASTOR'S POCKET LIBRARY

Mobile, Alabama

How To Find and Call a New Pastor
by Robert Strand
Copyright ©2015 Robert Strand

Scripture is taken from the Holy Bible, New International Version®, NIV® Copyright ©1973, 1978, 1984, 2011 by Biblica, Inc.® Used by permission. All rights reserved worldwide.

ISBN 978-1-58169-598-4
For Worldwide Distribution
Printed in the U.S.A.

Evergreen Press
P.O. Box 191540 • Mobile, AL 36619
800-367-8203
evergreenpress.com

Contents

Appendices –
Pastoral Search Forms   39

Introduction

Since "retiring" as a senior pastor, I have had the privilege of serving as an interim pastor in sixteen churches, large and small, in six different states and cultures. While serving as the interim, I have also had an exciting insider's view of the selection process. Also during this time, I have served as a consultant to walk the church board or selection committee through this important time in the life of a church.

While I was consulting with a small country/rural church, a board member asked, "Pastor, we are completely out of touch and ignorant of how to proceed and how to find and call a new pastor. Would it be possible to create an easy, simple, step-by-step plan of action for us to follow?"

This book is the result of such requests. From my experience, small churches, especially, don't seem to check out the character and integrity of candidates efficiently and suffer the consequences as a result. I have intended to share with you what has worked for many churches in the past and hopefully will work for you in whatever your situation may be.

There are a number of lengthy books on the market, and most church denominations have their own manual with many more hoops to jump through. My desire, however, is to simplify what can be a difficult and time consuming process.

Along with the body of material, I have included some forms that may prove helpful. These are included to fit in this size book, but they are also available on-line to be printed out, edited to your specific needs, and used as needed.

I am especially happy to share with you the form to use for requesting recommendations from references. In today's litigious world, many people are reluctant to give you an honest reference; however, this form can help you cut to the chase as it's not lengthy and can be answered by simply choosing a number, which is not so intimidating. (This was developed by my wife who is a "counseling" psychologist with great insight into the human psyche.) After three interviews, you will begin to have a profile of the prospective candidate.

Enjoy the process! Pray much! And may God bless you with His choice for your next pastor or other pastoral team member.

Bob Strand
Springfield, Missouri 2015

Chapter 1

Search Committee

Pastors, by and large, set the tone for their church. Their leadership tends to determine whether their church is seeking to move on in God or not. You can see how important the choice of the appropriate leader is for your church.

The selection of a new pastor, associate pastor, or key ministry head is one of the most important events in the life of a church. Care must be taken to remind each parishioner of the seriousness, sacredness, and holiness of this process being undertaken.

The pulpit committee or pastoral

search committee is the necessary link between the congregation and the organized quest for a new pastor or associate pastor. This committee must believe that God chooses a particular person for a particular time for a particular assignment in the life of each congregation.

During this process always keep in mind that there may be a great difference between the pastor whom God has called and the pastor the committee or the church may want to call! Therefore the committee members must be actively seeking the Lord so they can be aware of God's choice.

Call of the Shepherd

The Bible provides many references about the call of the shepherd and their responsibility to God and the church.

The "God-called" shepherd is...

- One who cares for the flock:

  But He made His own people go forth like sheep, and guided them in the wilderness like a flock (Psalm 78:52-53).

- One who defends the flock:

  But David said to Saul, "Your servant used to keep his father's sheep, and when a lion or a bear came and took a lamb out of the flock, I went out after it and struck it, and delivered the lamb from its mouth; and when it arose against me, I caught it by its beard, and struck and killed it (1 Samuel 17:34-35).

- One who leads the flock to rest:

The Lord is my shepherd, I lack nothing. He makes me lie down in green pastures, he leads me beside quiet waters, he refreshes my soul (Psalm 23:1-3).

- One who is accountable for the flock:

Every tithe of the herd and flock—every tenth animal that passes under the shepherd's rod— will be holy to the Lord. No one may pick out the good from the bad or make any substitution. If anyone does make a substitution, both the animal and its substitute become holy and cannot be redeemed (Leviticus 27:32-33).

In the villages around Jerusalem and in the towns of Judah, flocks will again pass under the hand of the one who counts them,' says the Lord (Jeremiah 33:13).

- One who keeps the sheep and goats separate:

All the nations will be gathered before him, and he will separate the people one from another as a shepherd separates the sheep from the goats (Matthew 25:32).

- One who waters and feeds the flock:

When all the flocks were gathered there, the shepherds would roll the stone away from the well's mouth and water the sheep (Genesis 29:3).

- One who keeps the flock together:

The gatekeeper opens the gate for him, and the sheep listen to his voice. He calls his own sheep by name and leads them out. 4 When he has brought out all his own, he goes on ahead of them, and his sheep follow him because they know his voice (John 10:4).

The Bible indicates the seriousness of how and how not to lead God's children who are the Church.

Keep watch over yourselves and all the flock of which the Holy Spirit has made you overseers. Be shepherds of the church of God,[a] which he bought with his own blood (Acts 20:28).

Be shepherds of God's flock that is under your care, watching over them—not because you must, but because you are willing, as God wants you to be; not pursuing dishonest gain, but eager to serve; 3 not lording it over those entrusted to you, but being examples to the flock (I Peter 5:2-3).

Of course there is no formula that will guarantee success in the pastoral selection process.

Four Basic Ministries of the Church

Another way of looking at the ministry of the pastor, or any key ministry leader, is to look at the basic ministries that characterize the life, worship, and work of your church and see how the individual fits into them:

• Preaching...

He said to them, "Go into all the world and preach the gospel to all creation" (Mark 16:15)

How, then, can they call on the one they have not believed in? And how can they believe in the one of whom they have not heard? And how can they hear without someone preaching to them? And how can anyone preach unless they are sent? As it is written: "How beautiful are the feet of those who bring good news!" (Rom. 10:14-15)

• Teaching...

Therefore go and make disciples of all nations, baptizing them in the name of the Father and of the Son and of the Holy Spirit, and teaching them to obey everything I have commanded you (Matt. 28:19-20).

- Evangelism...

  Keep your head in all situations, endure hardship, do the work of an evangelist, discharge all the duties of your ministry (2 Tim. 4:5).

- Stewardship...

  Bring the whole tithe into the storehouse, that there may be food in my house. Test me in this," says the Lord Almighty, "and see if I will not throw open the floodgates of heaven and pour out so much blessing that there will not be room enough to store it (Mal. 3:10)

  The Lord answered, "Who then is the faithful and wise manager, whom the master puts in charge of his servants to give them their food allowance at the proper time?" (Luke 12:42).

It's also important that the committee keeps in mind the cultural, religious, educational, ethnic, and economic background of the church and the surrounding area. These forces will have an impact and defining role on the future of the church in the community.

The bottom line question to ask is: How can our church and our new pastor, associate pastor, or key ministry leader meet these changing needs and times and culture?

Chapter 2

Preparatory Questions

As we have seen, the focus of this committee should not be: "What kind of a pastor do we really want?" but rather : "What kind of a pastor do we need? What kind of a pastor is God's choice for our leader?"

Therefore the responsibility of the search committee is to recommend a pastor, associate pastor, or key ministry leader that is spiritually focused, a mature person, and one who loves people and desires to follow God's leadership pattern.

With that said, the committee needs to understand that there will be different leadership styles to consider. Which one will best fit your church? Only you can decide, but decide you must before you can consider various individuals for the job.

Which of the following types of leaders are you looking for?

• The **passive leader** is one who goes along with the flow and doesn't rock the boat.

• The **motivational leader** is one who is able to stimulate people to dream about doing the impossible with God's help to enlarge their vision.

• The **team-spirit leader** is one who encourages every one to become involved for the benefit of all the church and community.

• The **authoritarian leader** is one who gives instruction, preaching, teaching, and leadership without compromise.

There are also many other questions for a new leader to be considered:

• What are their administration skills?

• Do they have organizational skills?

• Is there an ability to give sound guidance and mature counsel?

• Can the candidate give guidance to direct future expansions?

• What is their educational background and plans for continued education?

• Will this pastor be "bi-vocational" or completely focused on your church?

Words of Caution

• Don't actively identify the weaknesses of each candidate. Remember, there are no perfect people or pastors.

• Don't expect a pastor to change himself/herself once they are chosen as pastor.

• Don't expect a "Bible teacher" type to become a "fiery evangelist" type.

• Don't allow the issue of age to be the most important factor.

• Don't expect a pastor to lead the church down paths that they don't want to go or teach on issues that are questionable or principles they do not want to learn.

• Don't become mesmerized by the candidates' physical characteristics nor their resumé.

Compiling the List

When compiling the list of ministers who wish to be considered for the position, there are some fundamental questions the committee needs to answer.

- Is this person one whom we can respect as our spiritual leader?

- Does this person have a positive spiritual and faith in God?

- What kind of an example will be set before others, especially our young ones?

- How does this candidate handle their own personal financial affairs?

- What is their attitude toward the grieving, sick, needy, hurting, and shut-ins?

- Does this person have a compassion for the unsaved, for our lost community?

- Does this candidate have a good attitude about him/herself, others, and life itself?

- Does this candidate care about physical health and personal appearances?

• Is this candidate loyal to the church and the denominational organization?

• Does this candidate have his or her home in good order?

• Does this candidate plan to make a long term investment in our church?

• Will this candidate wear well and not become boring for the long-term?

There are two axioms this committee should always consider:

1) In regards to their responsibility to the congregation: an informed church will be a happy church!

2) In regards to their vetting each candidate, they must never forget that the best predictor of the future is the history of the past!

Ten Common Search Committee Mistakes

There are some important mistakes for the search committee to avoid as they begin the process.

1. Failing to check out a candidate's track record.

2. Requiring a unanimous recommendation from the committee on the candidate presented to the congregation.

3. Making a decision based on a first impression.

4. Choosing a candidate the committee wants rather than the one the church needs.

5. Choosing a candidate who cannot adapt to the local culture.

6. Failing to evaluate the church's true condition.

7. Choosing a candidate because they are either exactly like or exactly opposite the former pastor.

8. Evaluating the candidate's sermons based upon one they have chosen, rather than ones chosen by the committee.

9. Having a committee that is too large.

10. Failing to be discreet and to maintain total secrecy during the search process. (Adapted from *in search of a leader* by Robert Dingman).

Many of these suggestions can be used by a pastor, as well, as he or she helps the church find associate, youth, or children's pastors, which are equally important positions to the success of the church.

Chapter 3

Sixteen Steps

Most of the time, serving on a church board should be a relatively simple and routine type of duty. However that all changes when the board and search committee are called upon to find and call a new pastor. There will be no shortage of free advice!

This process can be very time consuming and a source of some stress and pressure. The key to success is to prayerfully and systematically seek the leading of the Lord and to be diligent in the process. However, there are no shortcuts.

Although there is not one single right way, the following is offered as a suggested plan and timetable that can help the committee make good progress. Of course, always begin each meeting of the committee with prayer and come together in an agreement of purpose!

Sixteen Steps to Calling a New Pastor or Ministry Leader

Step 1:
Select a pulpit search committee, if other than the church board, or by adding other members to the board. Out of the group, select a key person or chairperson as leader. Make sure each member has an understanding of the requirements of the church by-laws as to the process required for the pastoral selection.

Step 2:

Begin building a suggested profile of the next pastor using a survey of the church members. While doing this, also build a profile of your church that includes financial statements, mission statement, statistics, etc. (See the form "Some Things the Candidate Would Like to Know about Our Church" on Appendix K.)

Step 3:

Plan an all-church special meeting to bring the congregation up to date on the process of how the search will be done. Introduce the search committee as well as anyone who might be helping as a consultant. You may ask for some input from the congregation. (For this step you can use the form, "Invitation Letter or an "Announcement to Congregation" on Appendix B.)

Step 4:

An agenda for this meeting could include some pertinent questions or ask for congregational input using a survey form. (See an included sample survey on Appendix C.)

Step 5:

Tabulate the survey findings to use as a profile from the congregation. Have your first committee meeting to organize and begin. Should you decide to "call" a pastor who has not sent you a resumé yet, this is the time to ask! (Use the "First Board Contact Letter to Prospective Candidate requesting a resume" on Appendix H, but it's a courtesy to precede sending this letter with a short phone request.)

Make sure to ask for samples of their preaching/teaching ministry. You can request cds, dvds, a web site, etc. You may ask for three samples: one from a major holiday such as Christmas or Easter, another one would be the most current Sunday message they have given, plus one more message of his/her choice.

Step 6:

This is an on-going step to take. As each resumé is sent to you, it's a courtesy to send an acknowledgement. (Use the sample letter: "Resume acknowledgement letter" to allay lots of follow-up phone calls Appendix I.) If no sample messages are included in the package you receive, you may also request samples as per the previous step.

Step 7:

It's time to study the resumés you have received. Keep track of who has written and submitted each resumé. (To help in keeping track, make sure each committee member has a "Resume Screening Check-list" form for each resume to be evaluated on Appendix J) This may take some real time and contemplation. Perhaps copies of the resumés could be available to committee members to be able to work on them outside of committee meetings.

Then, as a committee, it's best to evaluate them together and select five of the top ones. You may have to do this more than once! You could also decide on a cut-off date for submitting more resumes'.

Step 8:

Begin calling references! Always be kind and gracious on the phone, but keep in mind that many of the references will only want to give you platitudes that are positive. We need to get behind these to the real truth.

After you have finished with this phone interview, end with a request, "Would you be so kind as to give me the name of another person who could give me another perspective on this possible candidate?" (In order to get at some real helpful answers, use the "Pastoral Search Committee Referral Questionnaire" on Appendix D. After only three different referrals, you will be able to detect a pattern. You will need one for each reference call made.)

Step 9:

In checking references, always call a home district office if there is one in your denomination. Ask to speak with the district superintendent or the assistant district superintendent or district secretary. You must be very persistent here to get some of the right answers. (Use the "Pastoral Search Questions for District Officers" on Appendix E.)

Step 10:

If all the references and the submitted materials check out positive, it's time to make the first voice contact with the candidate. This step is very crucial and vitally important.

You can select one committee member to do all the phoning at this preliminary stage so the comparison is "apples to apples" and not "oranges to apples." Or you can do this as a group with a speaker phone set up. If you make this a conference call, have one committee member do the talking and ask the questions while the rest observe and respond. (It'll be helpful to use the suggested "Phone screening questions" form in conjunction with the "Phone Screening Evaluation Check-list" on Appendix F.)

Time Out

Let's take a brief "time-out." Does this all seem like a lot of make-do work"? Are you getting tired, already? Remember this is likely the most important duty you will ever have as a board member or search committee member. It may seem like a lot of detail, but remember, you need to be committed to do the very best search that you are capable of doing. Do your due diligence so that in the end, the Lord will confirm His will and reward your church for years to come. What you are doing here and now will affect your church and community from here to eternity! God will bless and reward your every effort!

Step 11:

If you were not satisfied or would like another opinion from another group member, it's okay to call the candidate again.

Step 12:

After you have evaluated sermons and other materials, it's time to plan on doing an "in-person-visit" to one of their present church services. Please be thoughtful and careful. Will this be a surprise visit? Or will this be the time to ask the prospective candidate if it would be okay to make a discreet visit? Respect his or her wishes. If you do visit, don't send your whole committee! Send perhaps one or two couples, but don't come in together and sit together and visit about what is happening. Observe everything that is going on. After the service, compare notes, write down your observations and report back to your full committee.

Step 13:
Remember, it's all still great fun and a wonderful adventure! This is the point at which it is time to meet each candidate you are seriously considering, in person, for an entire committee interview. You may want to invite the candidate and spouse to meet at an agreed

upon neutral location. A suggested format, if there is time, would be to meet for dinner on a Friday night, spend the evening in getting acquainted, with nothing heavy discussed. After everyone gets a good night of rest, you can meet for breakfast and start with prayer. Plan to ask the heavy questions first and end with a brunch or lunch. You may also ask the candidate to close this time with a 5 or 10 minute devotional. Afterwards send the candidate on their way home.

Do not make a major commitment if you are not ready at this time! (You may still want to interview other candidates, for example.)

You should also give the candidate a complete a picture of your church and community: financial statements, mission statement, programming, numbers, area information, the pay package, and church facilities. (You may prefer to do this as a board-only time with your candidate.), Also make sure they have a copy of your church by-laws and constitution and understand the voting process.

Try to answer all questions for all parties involved. Again, it will be helpful if there is one spokesperson for the committee, although this will not preclude any other members taking part. Remember, we as a committee need to put our best foot forward too because the church will be under study by the candidate and spouse!

(You can use as a guide, "The Interview Between Candidate and the Committee" on Appendix G as well as the information you have gathered in "Some things the candidate would like to know about our church" on Appendix K.)

Plan to pay all out-of-pocket expenses for the candidate and spouse.

Step 14:

When you decide on the candidate to present to the congregation, as per God's leading, set the date for the "tryout weekend. Then pray as never before that this choice will be confirmed by the congregation!

A suggested schedule for the candidate and the church may look like this:

Friday:
- candidate and spouse should arrive early afternoon at the motel.
- set a time for dinner with entire committee and spouses.
- follow with an easy evening of fun

and get acquainted, no business.
- Saturday...breakfast together with a short devotional to begin the day.
- Begin at 9:30 am at the church for last interview with committee to answer any other questions.
- About 10:30 introduce all other church leaders, youth, Sunday school, women's, men's, etc. so the candidate can ask questions.
- Lunch time, tour facilities, tour town, more questions with leaders.
- 5:00 pm, provide a buffet supper for the entire church family. Plan this evening so all can meet the candidate and family. Allow time for questions and answers. In consideration of the candidate, this should not last longer than 8:30 or 9:00. The next day will be a huge day for all.

- Sunday am service should be conducted by the chairperson and worship group, unless the candidate prefers another format. The chairperson will introduce the candidate at the appropriate time. He or she should not be asked to do more than give the pastoral prayer and preach, unless they might prefer otherwise.
- The pm service could follow the am, or in this service, the candidate could be completely in charge and bring the message as well.

Be very clear to the candidate and the church as to when the vote will be taken—immediately following the Sunday pm service or at a specially called business meeting.

(Consult the by-laws and make

sure the proper announcements have been made to the congregation and candidate. Follow this by-law to the letter!)

Step 15:

Job well done! Well, not quite yet. If you have a positive vote and the call has been answered, make sure of the moving dates and any arrangements that need to be made. Finalize any outstanding questions. If a parsonage is part of the package, make sure it has a fresh face-lift—carpet, paint, needed repairs, etc.

Step 16:

The final touches! There is nothing more rewarding than participating in the process of the selection and election of a new shepherd in the church who will teach, preach, and lead the people of God to a new level.

- Please send a gracious letter to all the unsuccessful prospective candidate of thanks. (Use the form letter, "The no thanks letter" on Appendix L.)

- Upon the pastor's arrival: members of the board and search committee should be the first to meet, greet, welcome, and assist in the move to their new home!

- A publicity package should be prepared to announce the arrival of the new pastor. this should be given to all local media...tv, radio, internet, etc.

- The pastor's study/office at the church must be readied for an immediate occupancy, cleaned, painted, bookshelves available, desk, computer, and whatever else has been discussed with the new pastor.

- A welcome reception and congregational housewarming, complete with a grocery shower, will jump-start the process of developing trust, respect, and friendships for a long and fruitful ministry!

There is no formula that will guarantee absolute success in this pastoral search process. However, these suggested principles and procedures have been tested and should prove to be safe guidelines in the search for a competent and worthy pastor who will lead your church to a new level, in the ways of God.

Then, I will give you shepherds after my own heart, who will lead you with knowledge and understanding (Jer. 3:15).

Now you can breathe easier, it's done! Well, it's still not quite finished! Now it's your privilege to give your prayers and full support to your new pastor. Be loyal, loving, and grateful for God's gift to your church.

And together, your new leader, your church, your God, and you will see the hand of the Lord as you move to a new level in the kingdom of God!

To God be the glory, honor, and power forever and forever! Amen!

APPENDICES

Pastoral Search Forms

Feel free to copy or adapt these forms for your own use. You can also access editable versions of these forms online:

http://evergreenpress.com/pastoral-search-forms/
Password: rodonstrand

APPENDIX A
Congregational Survey

The purpose of this survey is to enable the Pastoral Search Committee to more accurately gauge the thinking of our congregation. When you express preferences and suggest options, the pastoral search committee will take them seriously as a guideline in searching for our next pastor. Please understand that the ultimate charge to the pastor search committee, however, is to find the will of the Lord in the search process.

Please return this survey no later than Sunday, ________________

Please check one in each statement.
I am: ____ male ____ female

My age is: ___12-19 ____20-39 ____40-59 ____60 and over

1. In my opinion, the minimum acceptable educational level of the new pastor should be:

____ less than a high school graduate

____ high school graduate only

____ attended some college

____ college graduate

____ attended some seminary

____ holds a master's degree

____ earned doctorate

____ seminary master's degree

____ seminary doctorate

____ formal education unimportant

2. The years of prior pastoral or professional experience preferred:

____ no prior pastoral experience necessary

____ five years or less

____ more than five years as lead pastor

____ more than ten years as pastor

3. In my opinion, the preferred age range for our new pastor is:

_____ no age preference

_____ 20 to 29 years

_____ 30 to 39 years

_____ 40 to 49 years

_____ 50 to 59 years

_____ 60 or more years

4. Would you wish the pastor search committee to give consideration to a candidate who: *(check all that apply)*

_____ is single

_____ is female

_____ is in the process of becoming a credentialed minister

_____ is retired

_____ has no children in the home

5. If the candidate is married, what should be the role of the spouse?

_____ a silent partner

_____ active partner in ministry

_____ supportive, not active in leadership

_____ doesn't matter

6. Please check what you consider to be the new pastor's top five ministry priorities:

_____ a gifted teacher who enables persons to learn and understand spiritual truth

_____ an administrator of the church affairs

_____ a person active in media and public relations of the church

_____ a person active in sectional and denominational activities and programs

_____ a community volunteer who cooperates in community activities

_____ an effective communicator with

well-prepared sermons

_____ a skilled counselor available to assist persons with personal problems

_____ a person who emphasizes evanglism, witnessing and outreach

_____ a person who will be home and foreign missions minded

_____ a person with leadership and a vision for the church's future

_____ a person who uses praise songs and or drama in worship

_____ a person who prefers to feature hymns and gospel songs in worship

_____ a nurturing leader who is growing personally and helping others to mature

_____ a person who emphasizes the importance of building strong families

_____ a person who emphasizes the importance of holy living

_____ a person who will be making personal calls on the sick and shut-ins

_____ a person who communicates well with children

_____ a person who communicates well with youth

_____ a person who communicates well with adults

_____ a person who communicates well with senior adults

_____ a person who communicates well with singles

_____ a person who communicates equally well with all ages

_____ a person who is willing to commit to a long-term pastoral ministry

Please feel free to express yourself on any other issues that are of importance to you:

____

____

____

____

____

____

____

Remember...we have a "search" committee, not simply a "receiving" committee of resumés. Do you have a suggestion of a possible pastor who currently is pastoring a church at the level we would like to be in five years?

____

____

____

APPENDIX B

Invitation Letter/ Announcement to the Congregation

Dear ___________________:

Greetings from your church board! With the recent resignation of our senior pastor, we are looking to a new era in the life of our church. We have a wonderful congregation that God has blessed for many years, and now we look forward to seeing what God has planned for us in the future.

We are going to take some time to look at our church and will be listening to you to tell us what you believe we should look for in our next senior pastor. We are interested in your opinions about how we can enhance the ministries we already have and what we need to do to become an even stronger witness in our community.

With this in mind, we invite you to join our board members for a very special meeting at the church at _______ pm on ______________. We are excited about the future and your help and God's direction.

Sincerely,
Church Board

APPENDIX C
Questions to Consider at Congregational Meeting

Note: this should be passed out at the begin-ning of the meeting so that everyone can have an opportunity to think about their answers during the discussion time. Take careful notes of each response and compile the answers for reference after the meeting has been com-pleted.

1) What do you think are the top two strengths of our church?

____

____

2) What attracted you to attend our church in the first place?

____

____

3) If you could change one thing about our church, what would it be?

____

____

4) What do you think we need to do to increase attendance at our church?

____

____

5) Are there any programs or ministries that you would like to see begun or enlarged?

____

____

6) In our search for a new senior pastor, what would you like us to look for?

____

____

APPENDIX D

Pastoral Search Committee's Questionnaire for References

Date: _______________________________

Pastoral candidate's name:

____

How long before now and in what capacity have you known this candidate?

____

____

Would you be so kind as to rate this person with respect to each of the characteristics listed? Please do so on a scale of 1 to 10. (1 is the poorest – 10 is the best). *Circle the appropriate number.*

1) Physical condition, health wise
1 - 2 - 3 - 4 - 5 - 6 - 7 - 8 - 9 - 10

2) Personality, charisma, being well liked by others
1 - 2 - 3 - 4 - 5 - 6 - 7 - 8 - 9 - 10

3) Intelligence—as good or above average
1 - 2 - 3 - 4 - 5 - 6 - 7 - 8 - 9 - 10

4) The ability to formulate, execute, and carry out plans
1 - 2 - 3 - 4 - 5 - 6 - 7 - 8 - 9 - 10

5) Leadership, the ability to inspire others and maintain it
1 - 2 - 3 - 4 - 5 - 6 - 7 - 8 - 9 - 10

6) Teamwork, the ability to work with different personalities
1 - 2 - 3 - 4 - 5 - 6 - 7 - 8 - 9 - 10

7) Well balanced and self-controlled.
1 - 2 - 3 - 4 - 5 - 6 - 7 - 8 - 9 - 10

8) Willingness to serve others
1 - 2 - 3 - 4 - 5 - 6 - 7 - 8 - 9 - 10

9) Humility
1 - 2 - 3 - 4 - 5 - 6 - 7 - 8 - 9 - 10

10) Wisdom in use and management of money
1 - 2 - 3 - 4 - 5 - 6 - 7 - 8 - 9 - 10

11) Strong administrative skills
1 - 2 - 3 - 4 - 5 - 6 - 7 - 8 - 9 - 1 0

12) Preaching, teaching, and mentoring skills
1 - 2 - 3 - 4 - 5 - 6 - 7 - 8 - 9 - 10

13) Is this person's family life healthy?
1 - 2 - 3 - 4 - 5 - 6 - 7 - 8 - 9 - 10

14) Is the spouse a positive asset?
1 - 2 - 3 - 4 - 5 - 6 - 7 - 8 - 9 - 1 0

If you were in our position, would you extend this person a call to pastor our church?

yes_____ no_____ undecided _____
maybe_____ prefer not to answer _____

Thank you! Could you give us another reference who might know this person and their contact information?

____

____

APPENDIX E
Pastoral Search Committee Questions for District Officers

Date:_____________

Pastoral candidates name:

____

Member of the following district:

____

Name of district officer questioned:

____

1) How long and in what capacity do you know this pastoral candidate?

____

2) How long has he/she been a member of your district?

____

3) Has this candidate ever gone through a rehabilitation program?

____

4) Is this candidate cooperative and supportive of district ministries and programs?

____

5) Has this person held or is holding any district leadership positions?

____

6) Describe the type of ministry this candidate emphasizes in their pastoral capacity?

____

____

7) Does this person support the district (with tithes) in accord with the by-laws?

____

8) Does this pastor support in prayer and financially missions?

____

9) Do they abide by the constitution and by-laws of the district council?

____

10) Does this pastor have a positive or negative impact on the churches served?

____

11) Has this person been forced to re-sign or been voted out of any church?

____

12) Would you give this person an un-qualified recommendation to pastor our church?

____

13) Is there anything else we should know about this candidate, positive or

negative, before we might issue a call to be our next pastor?

____

____

____

(Listed below are some tendencies, that, if present, may reduce the effectiveness of a pastor's work and witness.)

As you run these by the district officer, have them point out any of them that are applicable to the candidate:

impatient...intolerant...argumentative domineering...sullen...conceited...rash critical...easily offended...irritable discouraged...prejudiced...anxious humorless...inability to take a joke...

Phone Screening and Evaluation Checklist

Questions

These are to be used during the initial phone conversation with the candidate. We are attempting to get to know the candidate in this first voice contact. by asking a few lead questions. You should be able to tell the committee quite a bit about the person that is not mentioned in their resumé. Pay close attention to how they speak! Are they articulate? Do they dominate this conversation?

Based on this conversation, you should be able to form some general opinions about whether or not to go forward with this candidate. Unless you are certain this person is not a fit, it might be wise to have another committee member make a follow-up call with additional questions just to get another perspective.

1) Please tell me about your background. Where did you grow up? What schooling do you have? (Treat this like a conversation you would have if you are trying to make a new friend. Find common ground. Look for any gaps in the resumé so that you can fill them.)

____

____

____

____

____

2) What is your ministry history? (See if their story tracks with their resume. Don't be afraid to ask sensitive questions like, "Tell me why you left your last assignment." or "Describe your preaching style.")

____

____

____

____

____

____

3) Please tell me about your current ministry. (It's likely you will get a positive picture, which is good, but probe a bit beyond the obvious. Do ask about areas left out.) Describe the demographics of your town and congregation.

____

____

____

____

____

____

4) Ask for a few details about the Sunday school, youth group, senior adult ministries, children's ministries and the nursery. (Here we are probing to find out how much they are involved and engaged in the details of their church. Do they really know what's going on?)

____

____

____

____

____

5) Does your church have a website? If so, what role do you have to do with it? (Follow up by going to the website to see if it reflects the kind of emphasis you are looking for.) If no website, ask what other kinds of ministry outside of the church they may be engaged in. What else can you provide that would be a good example of their writing skills? (Note: usually a person's writing style reflects their speaking, research, thinking, and preparation.)

____

____

____

____

____

____

____

6) Why are you interested in pastoring our church? (Here you need to get past the "finding God's will" answer! Most everyone has a reason why they are looking for a new church assignment! Your job here is to find out what that reason is!)

____

____

____

____

____

7) (Always...be kind, courteous, & respectful! Remember your church is also being scrutinized!)

Phone Evaluation Checklist

This is to be used to evaluate the phone interviews. Evaluate each concept on a 1 to 10 scale. Be on the lookout for any "no" answers that could indicate a problem.

Date:_______________

Candidate:

____

______ (1) Does this applicant have a pleasant demeanor over the phone?

______ (2) When speaking about personal background, does the applicant speak with pride and confidence? Does the family life sound solid?

______ (3) When discussing ministry history, does the applicant express negative feelings toward any former churches or church boards?

_____ (4) Are all the gaps in the ministry resumé satisfactorily explained?

_____ (5) Does the applicant seem to be running away form something at his or her current situation?

_____ (6) Is the applicant "long winded" in their answers?

_____ (7) When describing the programs at his or her church, does the applicant demonstrate a working knowledge of each ministry or program?

_____ (8) Is this applicant able to clearly articulate their interest in your position, beyond simply "seeking God's will for your church."

_____ (9) Does the applicant ask good questions about your church?

______(10) At the end of your conversation, do you like the person and could you see yourself as a friend and their serving as senior pastor?

______(11) Does this applicant know anyone currently in the church?

______(12) Do you come away with a positive reaction and feel we need to take this to the next step?

Please note any other observations you may have made during this phone conversation:

____

____

____

____

APPENDIX G
Interview of the Candidate by the Committee

At some point in this process, there should be a healthy and free exchange of ideas between the parties. Here are some suggested questions:

1) Please tell us about your conversion, water Baptism, infilling of the Holy Spirit.

____

____

____

____

____

2) Tell us about your "call" to Christian and church ministry.

---

3) What is your belief about the Bible as the inerrant written word of God.

---

4) How much time do you spend weekly in sermon preparation?

____

____

____

5) What is your view of how a total balanced church ministry should work?

____

____

____

____

____

6) How can we as a church meet the challenges of the current day and time?

____

____

____

____

____

7) What is your attitude toward Christian education?

____

____

____

____

____

____

8) How do you see your relationship with church board, trustees, church staff, and department leaders in the ministry of our church?

____

____

____

____

____

9) List three strengths and three weaknesses of your ministry.

____

____

____

____

____

10) How do your spouse and children view your ministry?

____

____

____

____

____

11) If you care to talk about your children, what are some of their goals?

____

____

____

____

____

____

12) How would you involve yourself in our community?

____

____

____

____

____

13) What is your feeling toward church and how can it be attained?

____

____

____

____

———————————————

———————————————

14) Please tell us the history of your pastoral ministry and something about the churches you have pastored.

———————————————

———————————————

———————————————

———————————————

———————————————

15) List your life and ministry priorities and long term goals.

———————————————

———————————————

———————————————

———————————————

———————————————

16) Why would you like to become the pastor of our church?

____

____

____

____

____

____

17) Please tell us something unique about you or your family.

____

____

____

____

____

____

APPENDIX H
The First Committee Contact Requesting a Resume or More

Dear _____________________:

Christian greetings!

My name is _____________________ and I am writing on behalf of the Pastoral Search committee at

_______________________________.

Perhaps you have heard our senior pastor has resigned, and we are conducting a search for new pastor. Your name has been submitted as someone who we may be interested in talking to about this position.

After prayerfully considering this request, we would be please to receive a resumé from you. Along with the resumé, would you be so kind as to include three CDs or DVDs as examples of your preaching ministry? (One should be from a Sunday when celebrating a holiday, such as Christmas, Easter, July fourth; one should be of your last Sunday's service; and one can be of your choice.)

We will keep your information in strictest confidence as we explore together the possibility of a mutual decision. You may send the resumé to my attention at:

____

____

Thank you for considering serving the

_______________________________.

If you would prefer to discuss this with me prior to sending your resumé, please feel free to contact me at

_______________________________.

Sincerely,
Committee Member

APPENDIX I
Resumé Acknowledgment Letter

Dear _____________________:

Thank you for sending your resumé for the senior pastor position at

____

_____________________.

We will carefully review it to determine if it is a fit for our church. Meanwhile, please be patient with us as we review all the resumés we have received. We will be back in touch with you as soon as possible.

Please be praying with us for God's direction for everyone in this process.

Sincerely,

Committee Member

APPENDIX J
Resumé Screening Checklist

(This is to be used when reviewing resumés only.)

Date:_______________________

Candidate:

____

Reviewer:

____

______ (1) Is the resumé easy to read?

______ (2) Are all the words spelled correctly and correct English used?

______ (3) Does the resumé reflect a positive history of the candidate?

______ (4) Is there evidence of "job hopping"? Does the applicant move around a lot?

_____ (5) Are there any unexplained gaps in the work history?

_____ (6) Does the applicant speak negatively of any previous employers or churches?

_____ (7) Do the education and ministry experiences match up with your requirements?

_____ (8) Are you, the reviewer, familiar with any of the previous churches or references listed?

_____ (9) If a cover letter is attached to the resumé, is it professional in appearance and in content?

_____ (10) When compared to other resumes you have received, does this resume stand out in a positive way? Why?

____

____

____

____

____

______ (11) Should we give this applicant further consideration based on this resumé?

Please, would you as reviewer be so kind as to share any other thoughts or observations that would be important to you and the committee?

____

____

____

____

APPENDIX K
What a Candidate Might Like To Know About the Church and Community

This could also be presented as an "informational" packet. The following are some of the possible questions the pastor-elect may wish to ask or would surely appreciate knowing if we volunteered the following information. This is very important!

1) Share a short historical overview of church and community.

2) Explain about the church unity, the lay leadership, and congregation at large. Also, what were their relationships with previous pastors.

3) The number of board members or

trustees we have and how their ministry is working in our congregation.

4) Under what conditions did the previous pastor leave the congregation.

5) When/if you become the pastor, the freedom you will have to preach/teach the Word, as God, and the Holy Spirit may direct.

6) Here is what the congregation will expect of their pastor.

7) Here is a short overview and the relative health of each of the following programs:
- evangelism and outreach ministries
- Christian education
- youth ministries
- missions...foreign and home

- community social or outreach actions
- women's ministries
- men's ministries
- properties we have, assets we hold, debts we are servicing
- financial...budgets for the past five years, the financial health of the church

8) The plans and visions for the future.

9) The ministries that need immediate attention and improvement.

10) The salary package you are offering. (board & candidate only)

11) Any other questions would they like you to answer for them?

APPENDIX L
The "No Thank You" Letter

Dear _______________:

Thank you for sending us your letter (or other materials) regarding becoming our senior pastor here. We have carefully reviewed and discussed your information. While your credentials are impressive, we have decided to move in another direction in our search.

We are certain God has a specific plan for you and we wish you all the best as you seek His guidance for your life and ministry. We realize that the sharing of your information with us is a difficult decision and we do not treat it lightly.

Thank you again for your interest in our church.

Sincerely,
Committee Member

About the Author

ROBERT STRAND is the author of more than 60 books, and his "Moments To Give" series has sold more than a million copies. A consummate storyteller, Robert knows how to blend the emotional impact of true stories with practical insights from his many years of pastoral experience to produce breakthrough results. He and his wife, Donna, live in Springfield, Missouri.

You can download the forms in the Appendices at:

http://evergreenpress.com/pastoral-search-forms/
Password: rodonstrand

Other books by Robert Strand

Angel at My Door

The B Word

Breaking Generational Curses

In the Company of Angels

Desperate Housewives of the Bible—
Old Testament

Desperate Housewives of the Bible—
New Testament

Live Fully, Laugh Often

A Miracle Is a Miracle